A Refugee's Journey from

Nigeria

Ellen Rodger

CRABTREE
PUBLISHING COMPANY
WWW.CRABTREEBOOKS.COM

Author: Ellen Rodger

Editors: Sarah Eason, Harriet McGregor, Wendy Scavuzzo, and Janine Deschenes

Proofreader and indexer: Wendy Scavuzzo

Editorial director: Kathy Middleton

Design: Paul Myerscough and Jessica Moon

Cover design: Paul Myerscough and Jessica Moon

Photo research: Rachel Blount

**Production coordinator and
   Prepress technician:** Ken Wright

Print coordinator: Katherine Berti

Consultants: Hawa Sabriye and HaEun Kim, Centre for Refugee Studies,
   York University

Produced for Crabtree Publishing Company by Calcium Creative

Publisher's Note: The story presented in this book is a fictional account based on extensive research of real-life accounts by refugees, with the aim of reflecting the true experience of refugee children and their families.

Photo Credits:
t=Top, bl=Bottom Left, br=Bottom Right

Inside: Jessica Moon: p. 29b; Pixabay: Kriemer: p. 13; Shutterstock: Ah_fotobox: p. 17; Andromina: p. 14t; Bakdc: p. 29tr; CK.PRO: p. 6tr; d'Naya: p. 20b; Hennadii H: p. 20t; Jordi C: pp. 7, 19b, 25; Anthony Krikorian: p. 8t; Ivan Kuzmin: p. 12t; Macrovector: p. 3; David Mbiyu: p. 11t; MSSA: pp. 28, 29cl; Ariyo Olasunkanmi: p. 18b; VectorShow: pp. 18c, 19r; Kelsey M Weber: p. 5tl; UNHCR: © UNHCR/Hélène Caux: pp. 12b, 22b, 26; © UNHCR/Romain Desclous: pp. 15t, 22-23t; © UNHCR/Rahima Gambo: pp. 20bl, 27; © UNHCR/Francis Garriba: p. 21; © UNHCR/George Osodi: pp. 5b, 15b, 22-23b, 24; Wikimedia Commons: Shariz Chakera: p. 9t; GreaterHappy: p. 8b; Khamisuabubakar: pp. 20-21b; VOA: pp. 11b; 14c.

Cover: Jessica Moon; Shutterstock: Kamomeen.

Library and Archives Canada Cataloguing in Publication

Rodger, Ellen, author
     A refugee's journey from Nigeria / Ellen Rodger.

(Leaving my homeland)
Includes index.
Issued in print and electronic formats.
ISBN 978-0-7787-4688-1 (hardcover).--
ISBN 978-0-7787-4699-7 (softcover).--
ISBN 978-1-4271-2072-4 (HTML)

     1. Refugees--Nigeria--Juvenile literature. 2. Refugee children--Nigeria--Juvenile literature. 3. Refugees--Social conditions--Juvenile literature. 4. Nigeria--Social conditions--Juvenile literature. I. Title.

HV640.5.N54R63 2018   j305.9'0691409669   C2017-907650-7
                                                                                        C2017-907651-5

Library of Congress Cataloging-in-Publication Data

Names: Rodger, Ellen, author.
Title: A refugee's journey from Nigeria / Ellen Rodger.
Description: New York : Crabtree Publishing, [2018] |
   Series: Leaving my homeland | Includes index.
Identifiers: LCCN 2017054803 (print) | LCCN 2017057136 (ebook) |
   ISBN 9781427120724 (Electronic HTML) |
   ISBN 9780778746881 (reinforced library binding : alk. paper) |
   ISBN 9780778746997 (pbk. : alk. paper)
Subjects: LCSH: Refugee children--Nigeria--Juvenile literature. |
   Refugees--Nigeria--Juvenile literature. | Nigeria--Emigration and
   immigration--Juvenile literature.
Classification: LCC HV640.5.A3 (ebook) | LCC HV640.5.A3 R63 2018
   (print) | DDC 305.9/0691409669--dc23
LC record available at https://lccn.loc.gov/2017054803

Crabtree Publishing Company
www.crabtreebooks.com   1-800-387-7650

Printed in the U.S.A./022018/CG20171220

**Published in Canada
Crabtree Publishing**
616 Welland Ave.
St. Catharines, Ontario
L2M 5V6

**Published in the United States
Crabtree Publishing**
PMB 59051
350 Fifth Avenue, 59th Floor
New York, New York 10118

**Published in the United Kingdom
Crabtree Publishing**
Maritime House
Basin Road North, Hove
BN41 1WR

**Published in Australia
Crabtree Publishing**
3 Charles Street
Coburg North
VIC, 3058

What Is in This Book?

Leaving Nigeria

Nigeria is a land of contrasts, or differences. There is a small number of rich people who live in cities. But there is also a number of poor people. Their quality of life is much lower.

More than 186 million people live in Nigeria. There are about 500 different **ethnic groups**, but there are four main groups. Over the last 50 years, there has been a lot of fighting in Nigeria. There was a **civil war** for three years between 1967 and 1970. After that, the country was ruled by the military. The rulers kept the country's wealth for themselves. They also punished anyone who did not agree with them.

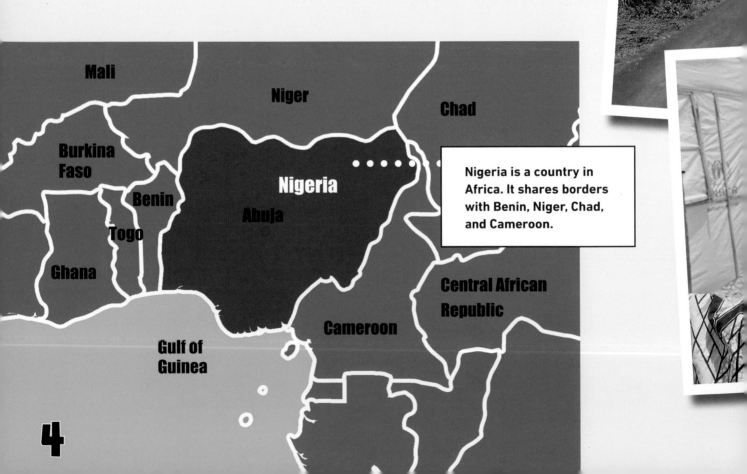

Mali

Niger

Chad

Burkina Faso

Benin

Nigeria

Abuja

Togo

Ghana

Central African Republic

Cameroon

Gulf of Guinea

Nigeria is a country in Africa. It shares borders with Benin, Niger, Chad, and Cameroon.

UN Rights of the Child

Every child has rights. Rights are privileges and freedoms that are protected by law. **Refugees** have the right to special protection and help. The **United Nations (UN)** Convention on the Rights of the Child is a document that lists the rights of children all over the world. Think about these rights as you read this book.

In Nigeria, the roads are very poor and difficult to drive on. It is not easy to travel around the country.

Many Nigerians have left their homes to escape violence. Some fled to neighboring African countries. They are refugees. Refugees flee their **homeland** because of unsafe conditions. Refugees are different from **immigrants**. Immigrants choose to leave to look for better opportunities in another country. Around 1.9 million Nigerians have fled their homes but remained in the country. These are **internally displaced people (IDPs)**.

Many IDPs live in camps like this one in northern Nigeria.

My Homeland, Nigeria

Nigeria is in West Africa. It has huge grassy plains, mountains, areas of rain forest, and swamp land. Its two main cities are Abuja and Lagos, but most people live in villages.

Many ancient **cultures** lived in Nigeria thousands of years ago. The people of modern Nigeria can trace their history back to these cultures. Today, more than 100 languages are spoken in Nigeria.

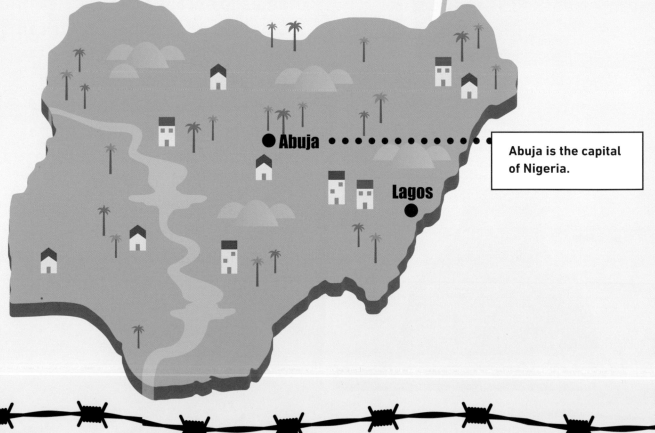

Nigeria's flag

● Abuja

Lagos

Abuja is the capital of Nigeria.

The three largest ethnic groups in Nigeria are the Hausa, the Yoruba, and the Igbo. The Hausa people live in the north. They follow the religion of **Islam**. This means they are Muslim. The Yoruba people live in the southwest. They follow **Indigenous** African beliefs. The Igbo people mainly live in the southeast. They follow the Christian religion.

Nigeria was controlled by Britain until 1960, when Nigeria became **independent**. But the different ethnic and religious groups in the government could not agree on how to rule the country. The southeastern part of Nigeria wanted to form its own country. This led to a civil war from 1967 to 1970. After the war ended, the country was still unstable. Today, the government finds it very hard to unite its many religious and ethnic groups.

Lagos is the largest city in Nigeria.

Nigeria's Story in Numbers

These are the largest ethnic groups in Nigeria.

Ijaw 10%

Others 26%

Igbo 18%

Hausa 25%

Yoruba 21%

Baseema's Story: Village Life

On summer nights when it was very hot, I liked to sit with my mother in our yard. I laid my head on her lap. I asked her to tell me about the night I was born and how my grandmother named me. My name is Baseema. It means "full of smiles." "You were happy from the minute you took your first breath," my mother said. I still like that story. It reminds me of good times and home.

I am the youngest of five children. My father was a leader in our village. He made decisions for people when there were disagreements. Because he had this duty, we often had people stay at our house. My father said it was important to treat our guests well and share the best food with them.

This Nigerian dish is called *bole*. Bole are roasted plantains, a type of banana. They are served with a pepper sauce and fish.

Nigeria has 36 states. Borno State is in northeastern Nigeria.

Our village, Baga, is in Borno State. My father helped set up our village school. Father believes education is important for the future. My school was just for girls. I went there with my sister Nafisaa, who is three years older than me. We are Hausa people.

Our house was big enough for my family and many guests. We lived there with my aunt, Dalmaa. Dalmaa liked to spoil us with treats such as masa, which are rice puffs. My older brothers are Umar and Abdullah. They study engineering and agriculture at the university in Maiduguri. My older sister Jameelaa lives far away, in the big city of Kano. She is married and has one child, which makes me an innaa (auntie)!

Nigeria's Story in Numbers

Nigeria's population is

50.8 percent Christian.

Borno State's population is

93 percent Muslim.

Boko Haram

Since the 1950s, there has been ethnic and religious violence between the Christian and Muslim groups. Nigeria is rich in **resources**, such as oil. However, the government was dishonest. It kept the resources for itself and left many people poor. Some turned their anger into violence.

In 2009, a group called Boko Haram began attacking people in northern Nigeria. They were **extremist Islamic terrorists**. At first, they targeted schools, police, and the army. But the violence spread. Boko Haram's view of Islam is not accepted by most Muslims.

Chibok

Nigeria

☐ Borno State

■ Areas controlled by Boko Haram

Boko Haram militants use violence to control parts of Borno State. The brown areas shown here are under Boko Haram control.

UN Rights of the Child

Children have the right to be protected from kidnapping. They have the right to be protected from being hurt or mistreated.

Thousands of people have been killed by Boko Haram. **Militants** attack quickly and burn villages. They also bomb markets and buildings in cities. They target schools with violence. They believe girls should not be educated, and target girls in schools, too. In 2014, Boko Haram kidnapped 276 girls from a school in Chibok, Borno State (see map). A few girls have escaped, and some were released in 2017. However, most are still missing.

People gather to speak out against the kidnapping of 276 Nigerian school girls.

#BRING BACK OUR GIRLS

ALL LIVES MATTER

Fathers of the missing girls grieve for their daughters.

Baseema's Story: Attacks and Violence

Every month, my father made trips to the city of Maiduguri to do business. Sometimes, he brought us with him. We visited my brothers. That all stopped when Boko Haram came to the city. They are a very violent terrorist group. My father does not believe what they believe. This is dangerous. They kill people who do not agree with them.

There are 30 million children of elementary school age in Nigeria. Children begin elementary school at age six.

Boko Haram attacks towns and villages in Nigeria. They bomb or burn stores, schools, homes, vehicles, and buildings.

There was so much fear. Boko Haram killed people in villages, at schools, and on the road. We were worried they would come to our village. Soon, they closed our school because it was not safe for us to be there. My father told us we could not leave our home. He was too afraid we would be taken by those very bad men. My father is a good man and he believes it is important for us to learn. He said it broke his heart to take us from our school. But the threat was too great.

We said goodbye to our teachers. The teachers fled to the city. They were scared, too. Our days were different after that. At home, Nafisaa helped my mother clean, tend the garden, and take care of the cattle and goats. My job was to feed the chickens, collect eggs, and help prepare meals. I did some school work in a workbook. I love math and reading. In my home, I was free but I did not feel free.

Families in rural Nigeria often keep their own animals for food.

Empty Villages

Northern Nigeria is a dangerous place to live. People are afraid. Boko Haram continues to kill and kidnap people. The government and military are fighting back. But the military has been accused of burning homes and killing people they believe to be supporters of Boko Haram.

Boko Haram has kidnapped thousands of people. Some, such as these women and children, have been freed by the Nigerian army.

Many schools were closed out of fear of attacks and kidnappings. Boko Haram believes that Western education should be forbidden. It has attacked many schools.

An estimated 2,000 women and girls have been kidnapped by Boko Haram in northern Nigeria.

1.2 million children

had fled their homes in northern Nigeria by 2015.

This town on the border with Cameroon was controlled by Boko Haram until the Nigerian army freed it in 2015.

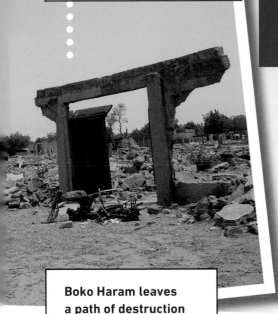

Boko Haram leaves a path of destruction everywhere it goes.

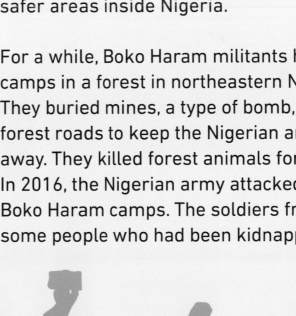

When the terrorist group attacks schools or villages, people flee in terror. Often, villages are burned to the ground so people cannot return. Thousands of refugees hope to find safety in the neighboring countries of Cameroon, Chad, and Niger. Others have gone to safer areas inside Nigeria.

For a while, Boko Haram militants had camps in a forest in northeastern Nigeria. They buried mines, a type of bomb, on forest roads to keep the Nigerian army away. They killed forest animals for food. In 2016, the Nigerian army attacked many Boko Haram camps. The soldiers freed some people who had been kidnapped.

Baseema's Story: Fleeing Terror

Nafisaa was milking our goats when my cousin came to tell her we must leave. One day before, Boko Haram drove into a village near us and attacked with guns. Many people were dead. They burned books and took the women and girls away. Now, my cousin could hear the buzz of Boko Haram motorcycles in the distance. He said we must all run for our lives.

My father was not home. He had gone to Maiduguri and was not back yet. My sister came running into the house saying, "They are coming, we must run!" Dalmaa snatched a blanket and some food. My mother did not even have her shoes when we ran. We left everything behind.

Baga

Maiduguri

Baseema's family hoped to reach the city of Maiduguri. It was 120 miles (193 km) away from Baga.

Boko Haram burn books because they do not support any non-Islamic education or knowledge.

The government must help ensure your rights are protected. They have a duty to help your family protect your rights, and help you reach your **potential**.

Boko Haram takes anything that is worth money, including animals.

We ran to the tall grass and hid. Our village was set on fire. The smell of smoke was strong. There were gunshots. Mother said we had to get farther away. We ran until we were so tired we could not stand up. We did not follow the road because it was too dangerous. We walked for a whole week. Dalmaa had brought yams (a root vegetable) and an onion in her blanket. They were not even cooked. But raw yams are better than dust and grass.

On the seventh day, we came to another village. The villagers took us in. They gave us their own food, even though they had very little to eat. My cousin and his family had escaped to the village, too. He told us that he thought we should go on to Maiduguri. My father was probably still there.

State of Emergency

For years, Boko Haram has attacked, bombed, and kidnapped people in northern Nigeria. Some people say that the government is not doing enough to protect people.

In 2013, the president declared a **state of emergency**. More troops were sent to the north. The government was given more power. In cities and towns, curfews were set. A curfew is a rule that tells people when they must stay indoors. People who went outside during curfew hours were arrested by police.

During a curfew, children are not free to play outside.

The state of emergency and curfews were meant to bring peace and security. But **human rights** organizations say they have made life even more difficult for Nigerian people. Many curfews last 24 hours or longer. These curfews can stop people from escaping during a Boko Haram attack. People cannot leave home to get food or go to work. The police have also been accused of arresting, beating, and killing people they believe support Boko Haram. Many people are kept in jail for long periods of time.

There have been an estimated **18,000 deaths** due to Boko Haram since 2009. There are no reports of the exact number of people locked up or killed by police.

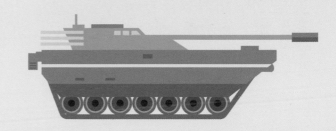

People cannot visit their church or mosque during a curfew.

Baseema's Story: Sheltering in the City

My cousin helped us get to Maiduguri. I was so happy to see my father and brothers! My father was overjoyed. He had heard news that our village was attacked. He was afraid we had been kidnapped or killed. We were so lucky that our family was together. This is not usual. Altogether with my cousin and his family, we were 14 people.

People flee to cities, such as Maiduguri, where they have family members who can help them.

Goats are important animals in Nigeria. They are traded at markets such as this one.

UN Rights of the Child

Children have the right to help from the government if they are poor or in need.

My brothers lived at the university, so we could not stay with them. Instead, my father's business friend let us stay with him. My cousin and his family went to stay with his wife's family. With our home gone, we lost all of our cattle and goats. That was most of our money. There was very little work for my father.

Families are often split up when they flee from Boko Haram.

My father did not think he could keep paying my brothers' school fees. Umar had almost finished his engineering studies, but Abdullah had two more years of study. My mother has a brother living in America and some cousins in Italy. My father asked if they would help pay for Umar to finish school.

Where Is Safety?

Attacks on villages and cities have increased in northern Nigeria. To escape the violence, people flee. They often walk to safety. IDPs live in camps within Nigeria. Others stay with family or friends who take them in. A smaller number of Nigerian refugees have crossed borders into neighboring African countries. All of these people are unable to go back home. This is because their homes are gone, or because Boko Haram may still harm them.

Some refugees are forced to return to Nigeria from camps in Cameroon.

Thousands of Nigerian IDPs live in Bakassi camp in Maiduguri.

1.8 to 1.95 million
people are IDPs in Nigeria.

205,815 Nigerians
are refugees in neighboring countries.

Most IDP camps are in the northern states where Boko Haram is most active. This makes IDP camps a target for attacks. The camps have tents for shelter. People have lived in them for many years. Some are run by charities and churches. At these camps, IDPs are given a little food and water. Many people become sick. The violence has destroyed normal life. Fewer people are farming and working. Food is hard to find for everyone.

Boko Haram militants have also spread into Cameroon, Niger, and Chad. This means people who flee Nigeria might not find safety in neighboring countries. **Host countries** have forced some refugees to return home. However, this is not allowed by law.

Children and adults carry water in this IDP camp in Maiduguri, in northern Nigeria.

Baseema's Story: An Uncertain Future

Life is very difficult. We have lived with our hosts in Maiduguri for three years. They are great hosts. Just like my father was when we lived in our village. We help out as much as we can, cooking and cleaning. It is not easy to care for two large families.

There have been many bombings in our neighborhood. A mosque close to us was bombed, and we were put under curfew. None of the women could go out of the house, anyway. Boko Haram kidnaps women and girls.

Young women and teenage girls are especially vulnerable to Boko Haram attacks.

UN Rights of the Child

Children have the right to education and the right to have people listen to and respect their views.

Women may be in danger when they leave their homes.

We have been blessed in other ways. My mother's family sent money for Umar to finish school. There was not enough for Abdullah to continue. He is with us now. Umar has a job in the city of Kano. Umar's earnings help support us. Several months ago, he came to get Dalmaa. They live with Jameelaa and her family now. Soon, we will all join them.

We do not know if we will ever go back to our village. That makes me very sad. My father wants Abdullah to return to school when we go to Kano. I am hoping that I can go back to school, too. Nafisaa thinks it is too late for her. Three years is a long time to be away from school.

The Struggle Continues

In many areas of the world, people are surrounded by violence and terror. The fighting makes everything difficult. People fear for their lives. It is a fear that does not leave them, even if they escape the danger.

Nigerians in IDP camps worry about their safety. Many of them are women and children. There is little food. Many areas are not safe from Boko Haram. This makes it difficult for aid organizations to bring food and water. Some aid organizations provide medical care. They also support people who have been kidnapped and harmed by Boko Haram. Some camps have built temporary schools. The **United Nations High Commissioner for Refugees (UNHCR)** works in IDP camps in Nigeria. It provides shelter and clothing, and helps IDPs find a safe place to live.

Nigerian IDP families do not always feel safer in the camps.

Many Nigerians live with family or friends. But this is difficult. There is often not enough money and food for large families living together. IDPs have lost their ways of life. They have also lost their homes and feelings of safety. These are things that cannot easily be replaced. Finding new work is also difficult.

Outside the country, Nigerian refugees face an uncertain future. Many have been forced to return to Nigeria from refugee camps in neighboring countries. If they do not have a safe home to return to, they are sent to IDP camps inside Nigeria.

Nigeria's Story in Numbers

198,322

Nigerian refugees were in neighboring countries in 2017.

Almost

7 million

people in northern Nigeria need aid such as food and medical supplies. This number includes people who are still living in their villages.

More than 12,000 refugees returned to Nigeria from Cameroon in May 2017.

You Can Help!

There are many things you can do to help newcomers and refugees in your community and elsewhere. Here are just a few ideas.

☑ Learn about Nigeria and the many different people who call the country home.

☑ Welcome refugees if they go to your school. Introduce yourself and tell them about your interests. Ask them about their interests.

☑ Take newcomers on a tour of the community. Show them where to find places such as stores and schools.

☑ Research aid organizations that help IDPs in Nigeria. Participate in or set up fundraising activities. Donate the money to the aid organization of your choice.

☑ Take part in World Refugee Day on June 20 every year.

☑ Share with your friends and family what you have learned about refugees in this book.

AID

People can help refugees by showing their support for them.

Discussion Prompts

1. Why are people fleeing areas of northern Nigeria?
2. What is the difference between an immigrant, a refugee, and an internally displaced person?
3. How would you feel if you were a refugee and had to leave your home, friends, and family members?

Glossary

civil war A war between groups of people in the same country

cultures Groups of people who have shared beliefs, values, customs, traditions, arts, and ways of life

ethnic groups Groups of people who have the same ethnic or religious origin

extremist Islamic Someone who supports extreme views in the Muslim religion

homeland The country where someone was born or grew up

host countries Countries that offer to give refugees a home

human rights Privileges and freedoms that all people should have

immigrants People who leave one country to live in another

independent Free from outside control

Indigenous Referring to people who have lived in a region for a long time, or are native to it

internally displaced people (IDPs) People who are forced from their homes but remain in their country

Islam The religion and faith of the Muslim people

militants People who hold extreme views of religion or politics and use violence to support these views

potential The best that someone is able to achieve

refugees People who flee from their own country to another due to unsafe conditions

resources A natural supply of something, such as water, oil, or plants, that can be used by people

state of emergency When a government takes away people's rights to regain control of an area

terrorists People who use violence to achieve a political goal

United Nations (UN) An international organization that promotes peace between countries and helps refugees

United Nations High Commissioner for Refugees (UNHCR) A program that protects and supports refugees everywhere

Learning More

Books

Achebe, Chinua. *Chike and the River.* New York, NY:
Anchor Books, 2011.

Seavey, Lura Rogers. *Nigeria* (Enchantment of the World).
New York, NY: Scholastic, 2016.

Thoennes, Kristin. *Nigeria* (Countries of the World).
North Mankato, MN: Capstone Press, 2016.

Websites

http://easyscienceforkids.com/nigeria
This site has information on Nigeria's location, its size and history, as
well as fun facts and vocabulary.

www.factmonster.com/people/kids-around-world/kids-nigeria
Read up on how kids in Nigeria live and play.

www.unicef.org/rightsite/files/uncrcchilldfriendlylanguage.pdf
Learn more about the United Nations Convention on the Rights
of the Child.

Index

About the Author

Ellen Rodger is a descendant of refugees who fled persecution and famine. She has written and edited many books for children and adults on subjects as varied as potatoes, how government works, social justice, war, soccer, and lice and fleas.